PATHWAYS

AuthorHouse™
1663 Liberty Drive
Bloomington, IN 47403
www.authorhouse.com
Phone: 1-800-839-8640

Published by AuthorHouse   05/29/2013

ISBN: 978-1-4817-4287-0 (sc)

Library of Congress Control Number: 2013907167

Acknowledgment

I am indebted to many people who have made this book possible. To my husband Gene A. Willliams, Cassandra, Deborah, Alicia, Kyle, Asia, Amari, and "to the only wise God, through Jesus Christ, to whom* be the glory forever! Amen.

Romans 16:27

Table of Contents

IT HURTS 1

No woman has a monopoly on this kind of man. 2

FOR A BOTTLE OF PERFUME AND SHIRT 4

WHO IS THIS MAN? 6

Not Willing to Give 7

A SKETCH OF A MAN 8

AND SUDDENLY YOU 9

The Dozen 10

We Women need to stick together 11

Freedom from Him.. 12

NEVER SAD 13

THE HOUSE THAT VICTORIA BUILT 14

Excuse Me.. 15

Honey I have a degree in this field 16

IKE ISON DOCK HENRY 17

WHY? 18

I was tired of pain 19

Life was beautiful while I lived it. 20

My child was a child who acted like a child............. 21

Life is energy.. 22

DEATH? 23

Barefeet 24

I'll Remember 25

CUT WOUND.. 26

BOUT WITH POLIO 27

POLITICAL LITERACY 29

YOU 31

Do This 32

FAKE! 33

ORDER! 34

RESPECT! 35

SPOTS . . . PLACES! 36

PEACE! 37

LEADERSHIP! 38

RISK! 39

DISCIPLINE! 40

BENEFITS AS A TEACHER 41

I AM CONCERNED 43

WHO KNOWS 44

MY FRiEND 45

Asia Wrote 46

I LOVE 47

I LIKE 48

Grabs My Mind 49

You Made Me Wonder 50

Not Sure 51

FEAR FEVER (SNAKES) 52

LOVE IS THIS 53

Im Excited 54

Im Fascinated By 55

Being late is A Habit 56

The Friendly Gossiper's Interview 57

The Call 58

Others 59

YOU 60

LONELY TEARS 61

How to lose a Friend... 62

Believe 63

WAS NOT WAS IS 64

WHAT IS DEATH... 65

Waited... 66

LADAKA.. 67

IT HURTS

To not see you again
To not hear your voice
To not feel your touch ever again
It hurts too much not to know where you are
What you're doing
Are you afraid, unhappy sad?
The finality of it all
Knowing you will never see them ever again
If we could just master this part . . .
Death would not be so terrifying.

No woman has a monopoly on this kind of man.

None of us women have a monopoly on this kind of
man.
He's out to get you and drive us insane.
The one who lies out the side of his mouth.
And winks at your very best girlfriend
As soon as you turn your head.
The one who cheats the same day you're married
Or the very next night
The buddy friend who needs a ride
Instead it's a woman by his side
The late hours of supposedly work
Just might turn out to be the night clerk.
The business trips you're never invited on.
None of us women have a monopoly on this kind of
man

We women need to stick together to keep our love
life better.
Abuse and pain we need not share
if for the married one we would not be there.
If the other woman would consider the wife
And think what if that was my life.
Say I don't need to help make her life more
miserable

I need to make this man be more
Considerable of his responsibilities,
None of us women have a monopoly on this kind of
man
Obligations and vows just don't be available
For him at another woman's expense.
Make it hard for him to be a whore
We women need to stick together.
relationships would be better.

FOR A BOTTLE OF PERFUME AND SHIRT

Ladies we give our man away for a bottle of perfume
and a shirt
Now gather around and listen to what I say
It's going to take a strong woman to not hurt
She found the shirt in the bottom drawer tuck away
underneath some other stuff
She asked the question where did it come from
He said I thought that you bought it.
You know you didn't but what's a lie
It's told to you all the time you say I did not buy this
now where did you get it from
Oh I forgot I bought that one from Momeka she sells
that stuff now.
That's it I'm out of here Momeka can have you.
You leave file for a divorce.
Momeka bought him for a bottle perfume and a
shirt—
You caught him with Momeka more than once
And now you will give him to her
Listen to this if he works and takes care of home
Then I'll buy him for 2 bottles of perfume and 2
shirts—give him to me.
I say keep your man
Here's how you handle Momeka.

You know where she works. Go there and order a
sandwich and coffee
Say "Momeka look what my husband gave me"—
You cut the shirt sleeve off at elbow roll them up
Spray the perfume all on you.
This is the shirt I've wanted go with my jeans
And don't you just love this scent.
When I find out where he got it
I'll let you know—get you some.

WHO IS THIS MAN?

When love is gone what do you do?
Do you keep on hoping feelings will ease?
What happened to the love that was here?
Maybe there was only one love the other pretend.
Some seem to think everyone is blind
that they can't be seen.
You must just hear
The signs were there from the beginning the
Hidden agenda did slowly appear.
No communication just let things be that way
I'm clear to do ill deeds and call any discussions an
argument
I don't have to face up to hear your needs
Why I'm good at turning pebbles into stones
I can turn the situation around to your
exaggerations and stretched out facts
Will make you look like the enemy too.
I can undermine I've did it before you
Women are no match for me
I've got this closet agenda the real me is very hard
for you to see.

Not Willing to Give

I don't even like you girls
What love is gone there never was any
Just pinch me
and I'll really tell. My desires
will blow your mind. "Oh well"
If I don't talk I can hide the real person.
I'm ready to own a man without concern
of how you fell and the love you had that is gone
You helped me up I'll put you down
I want what I'm not willing to give,
not your name on what I have but my name

A SKETCH OF A MAN

Whatever you see on the outside
Is all there is to this man
Bling and a three piece.
suit.
Lots of talk with no substance
Not sincere just wants to score.
Nothing is there but a suit of clothing, chains and
earrings
No man . . . not even an aging boy.
Just a sketch of a person
Taking up space and trying to perpetrate being a
man.

AND SUDDENLY YOU ...

I was surrounded by people all the time.
Alone, hungry for a special care.
And suddenly you.
We met, we touched, our hearts pounded.
We talked;you called.
And suddenly you.
We embraced, our eyes touched, we loved.
We smiled;we parted.
And suddenly we knew.

The Dozen

I have been living with about a dozen women.
Some are very pretty, clever, and fun to be with.
Some are vain, lazy and superficial.
One of them has three children and she tries
desperatly to be a mother to them.
One is kind hearted and practical.
One is gorgeous but cold selfish and grasping.
One is hungry for sex most of the time.
One is a total space case. And at least two of them
are prize
Bitches.
We all get along quite well actually
Considering what close space we have been forced
to occupy
The inside of my head

We Women need to stick together

To keep our relationships from abuse and pain
We need not have to share.
If the married one would not be there.
If the other women would consider the wife
And think what if that was my life
Think I don't need to help make her life more miserable
I need to make this man be more considerable.

Freedom from Him

Too much perhaps I think I loved him.
I was so completely dependent on him my breath
was drawn from him.
My strength was the off shoot of his vitality.
It was as if my whole personality was nothing more
than the sum total of my response to him.
He possessed a strange manipulative power over
me. At time I think he derived some sort of perverse
pleasure from making me suffer and jump like a
puppet on the end of a string.
Sleepless nights I have lain awake thinking of the
hurt he caused me. I remember how I cried about
the first women he cheated on me with; the second
one, the third one and with the tenth one . . .
I did not cry.
I know now what the thing was that started to grow
within me.
Freedom from him. Perhaps I could have forgave
him
for the cheating that has haunted my life from the
beginning of our relationship
But will I ever forgive for the whipping he gave my
spirit. I will carry the scar on my soul for the rest of
my life.
God has help me heal. I am free from him

NEVER SAD

Woven loosely in my heart
Room for hurt and pain to enter
God help me to tighten
These places, that tender
Life for me is simple, Not things make me happy, a
smiles, a touch, a kind
Word makes me so glad.
A fish jumping, a butterfly, a flower smelling of
perfume and I'm never sad.
Hoping for peace and contentment.

THE HOUSE THAT VICTORIA BUILT

The down payment had been made.
The house was completed, new from the ground up.
Victoria moved in. She was happy.
She soon discovered some exterior damages.
She had the repairs done. She was happy again.
Oh no, damage again. This time it was the interior.
Major Structural Damage. She called in the
Professionals. Each specialized in his field.
In spite of the repairs they made, they could not fix
everything.
The damage was too
Great and had spread. Victoria had to make a
Decision, whether to keep repairing or move.
The cost would be enormous either way. She
Loved this house and loved the people about
Her. It would be a painful decision to those
Who loved her. She moved. Perhaps the next
House would be in better shape and need less
Repairs.
Victoria died. She was 3 months old.

Excuse Me

I unlock the door.
I get there early enough so that the building is
accessible for use in the morning.
Lessons take the lead and young adults get ready
For a mass ball of skills thrown at them for
immediate mastering.
Ryan walks in lazily, looks around to see which
textbook is in use, grabs the book,
Sits next to Kyle.
Asks about the page and begin to talk on topics only
known to him and Kyle.
As I made my way threw the classroom chatter,
books thrown down,
Pencil sharpener making its fast spins. I enter
and say "Excuse Me !"quietness comes over the
classroom and pages start to turn.

Honey I have a degree in this field

My first year I believed a few,
Hurry I'm late . . . got a run to make
Time just slipped away baby
I'm sorry your birthday card is a day late
The second year I took white lies and smeared
lipstick,
Car trouble, coming into the door
I had four flat tires and I'm tired tonight.
My third year I took lying, wrong number calls.
Drive bys and named me Judy while making love
Forget our anniversary.
That's no place for you.
I don't like that movie,
I just don't have time.
My senior year I'd had enough
I took my clothes, my books,
My car, my selfrespect, and moved on.
I'm now working on my masters in my fate and on a
happier life.
I got a degree in that field

IKE ISON DOCK HENRY

But he was daddy to me.
Big strong a leaning statue of a man
Long arms a swaying back and a big hands.
Was this man working the land?
Hunting the woods and fishing the lakes taking care of
Things he grew and things he made was this man
call Ison
"Come here dock let me tell you about those
chillens" would call his Aunt Ella
"I'm not eating nothing till Dock come she told
daughter was the man called Dock
A man to deal with easy and giving never to argue,
Not to quick to anger but pushed in a corner this
man Henry was not to tangle.
But he was daddy to me.
Promising to let me put my new shoes on if I let him
remove a thorn from my foot.
A pat on my head.
A protective guy a big smile on his face bangs of hair
that stood up in the front, his left
Arm always slightly bent the right arm swinging,
A book that was far away a few words spoken to himself
From up the road or from the splashing of water in
the slew or a far of whistle coming toward
You. One could see or hear this man
Who was and will be daddy to me.

WHY?

How unfair it must seem.
why did it happen to my child,
Why did my child have to be in that place at that
exact time why?
The answer is not known
Take solace in that you were blessed with
Your child for however many years.
Did you ask why that particular child came through
you?
Did you ask who made the choice?
Look at you were chosen to be mother and father.
And take comfort there we aren't given a guarantee
on how long
we keep them.
Nor a warranty if there is a breakdown or
non-functioning part.
Remember the time you had with your child.
Look forward to the time you have left and think
I'm blessed.

I was tired of pain

It was driving me insane.
Perhaps death holds
Another page of life to unfold
Weep not.
For me worry neither for I may be in
A better place you see
Where I am or how things are I can't tell
All you can do is
Wish me well.

Life was beautiful while I lived it.

I had many experiences
I would not trade.
I shared my life with many.
Giving, taking, worrying, advising
those who came and went.
My time was well spent.
Life is like an air bubble.

My child was a child who acted like a child

He played, laughed, joked,
And got in mischief as a child will do.
Never should we forget that children
are on loan as we all are.
Paying off the loan is the living
When that loan is paid death takes over.
He is mine said the Lord.

Life is energy.

Energy cannot destroy.
The body is a house where the energy lives
As comfortably as can
When the house is no longer livable
All must move to another house
Hopefully more stronger and comfortable than the first
Enjoy your new home mother.

DEATH?

The mystery of death is the fear
The fear we have of not knowing
No one will ever tell
Is there heaven or hell?
If someone would only return
And ease other minds
What is experienced in that mystery called death?

Barefeet

Barefeet for the first years of my life.
could only wear shoes on Sunday.
Only one pair lasted on burn soles of feet.
When I grow up I will own 365 pairs.
I owned up to 205 before I realized
They were just things
Did not make me who I was
I still had only one pair of feet

I'll Remember

You were here this morning
you awoke with sleep in your eyes, stretching
You smiled at me and
You talked and walked out.
I remember the way you stared.
But not this evening you're all stretched out now.
And sleep will remain in your eyes.
You're not smiling now but I remember it well.
You're not talking now
I'll remember how.

CUT WOUND

On right thigh was cut
with a jagged can
While playing in mud with cousin Catherine.
Soot and lard was put
on it until it healed—left a 3in keloed.

BOUT WITH POLIO

I was diagnosed with polio at the age of 5
I could not walk
Could not stand for long
I had been taken from my grandparents by my real
MOTHER.
I had always believed my grandparents were my
mama and daddy
I did not want to leave.
I thought I would die if I had to leave to live with a
stranger
But mama and daddy made me go anyway.
Soon after I got there in about three days
I could not walk so I was taken to the two doctors.
Each said I had symptoms of polio
I needed another doctor who I later discovered was
a specialist.
After he examined me and ran test after test
He found nothing wrong.
So he asked me where the pain was.
I told him I didn't have any.
Can you stand up: No.?
When did you first notice you could not stand,
Right after I came live with Bill.
Who is Bill?
Mama and Daddy said that was my real mama.
Do you like living with her: NO.?

Do you think if I were to let you go back and
Spend some time with mama and daddy
You could stand up! I said yes.
So I stood up.
If I let you go stay with them would you walk for me!
Yes. So I walked.
And daddy took me back home the only home I
knew.

POLITICAL LITERACY

Why do we as citizens expect more from the people
Who run our schools than we do from the people
who run our cities?
From these public servants (teachers, principals,
etc) we expect qualified and trained
Knowledgeable, accountable, responsive and
responsible people.
From our political public servants we expect and
accept
Nothing more than a citizen being a long-time
member of an organization or community.
They run our city and thousands of dollars in
budget.
They are not required to have any experience or
knowledge of handling large amounts.
No knowledge of the structure and function of
government and no political literacy.
Political literacy a phrase I've coined to mean
Understanding of terms and vocabulary relevant to
the political process.
And being able to analyze key issues, study new
political ideologies and demand responsive and
responsible leaders.
We are experinceing difficulty in selecting and
electing political leaders
because of the above situations.

It is ironic that our children and teachers go through years of training to
Be governed by the untrained. They (teachers) required to have knowledge in the subject areas. They (political leader) should at least be required to be educated, articulate and politically literate.

YOU

You stand to long in one place you begin to sink
You stop and look back something may catch up
with you
If you're not in the line of fire don't step in it
You see today you and I spending
may not be the you and I of tomorrow
trying to create

Do This

Unless we do this
We are going to pay
We need to recruit—we need to foster
We need to encourage we need to keep
Our young people a program for their generation
Our generational programs are not working by
themselves
There is somewhat of an intimidation of labeling
and judging them fixing have to be optimistic
We got to believe things can get done better
Can't invest to much

FAKE!

Go to heaven or Go to hell.
This is what our prosperous spiritual leaders all tell
Fake!
Wait for the stars in your crown
Be good, Don't sin, you'll be back around
Fake!
They service funerals and handle the wake
they pass the cup on each occasion and count the
money they make
Fake!
The man gave the word
give more salvation promises
Keep them mournful sorrowful and hopeful more
than before
Break the leaders
lead before the followers heed
get the bullets going

ORDER!

Learning is compromised for order.
Learning in the classroom has become a by product
of order.
I began to feel that if I can just get some order,
learning has to follow.
I wonder if its not the other way around,
the order I get is the by-product of real learning
that will satisfy the students curiosity,
enthusiasm and in turn hold their interest.

RESPECT!

One of our most important and cherished
achievement of democracy
is our learning to have as much respect for the
personality of the child
as with the personality of the adult.
With a greater consideration for their feelings, needs
and interests,
real progress will come when all adults can
recognize that each child is different
and that all behaviors is caused.
Before we as parents and teachers can help our
children
with their emotional development.
We must understand something of ourselves.
The kind of person and adult is constitutes to a great
deal of
what he can do for a child.

SPOTS . . . PLACES!

We have many spots and places in our life.
Who fills those spots and places is usually up to us.
We may choose people
for some we may choose animals for some . . .
but the one spot or place for unconditional love and
support
is usually part full and part empty.
There is one person that usually fills the whole
spot . . . that person is mother.
Mother have one goal for their children . . . They
want the best.

PEACE!

The secret of peace is not to make our achievement equal
to our desires but to lower our desires to the level of our achievements.
It is useless for the individual will to fight against the universal will.
Slave pleaded in mitigation by the slave master own philosophy
he had been destined from all eternity to commit this fault
slave master replied had been destined to beat him for it.
Stoic thought—apathetic acceptance of defeat
Epicureanism—forget defeat in the arm pleasure
theories as to how one might yet be happy though subjugation.

LEADERSHIP!

Look upon an orchestra
where members are equally gifted and experienced
on his choosen instrument.
They each play a different beautiful piece of music
together during the same time.
With no one to gather and group these fine
musicians and channel their energy
skills and dreams
can you see the then noise.
Someone has to take into consideration
how each person with their talent work
and be able to combine, place, and structure
them into successful team effort.

RISK!

And old fellow very close to me once said
"If you play for more than you can afford to lose you
stand to gain".
Understanding a business venture that's a stretch
from my profession is a risk.
I've found that when I'm tough situation and pushed
against a wall,
I'm forced to perform and I do.
When I take on a challenge
I measure up my experience,
my strength, physical and mental health
and stack them up against the challenge
and go for it.

DISCIPLINE!

Another important factor
is not to give into things that doesn't matter.
There will be many voices of potential failure under
your voice.
Instead stick to what you are doing get through it,
complete it, survive it, whatever the situation.
Steer clear of the negative year toward the positive.
It's simply a matter of transcending.
When I'm tired and have pushed the edge of my
comfort zone,
I often think I'll close and go home,
but instead I push that comfort zone and keep
going.
The longer I do this
the more I realize I can do it.
I work anywhere from 60 to 78 hours most weeks.

BENEFITS AS A TEACHER

What makes it all worth
is you say I see a beam, eyes lighted, a blush or tears
subsided.
A child face when it beams pride of success
when a project has been completed or when he
finally grasp the meaning of factors
and says oh I get it it's like how many numbers you
can times together to get fifteen.
So those are factors a pupils eyes lighted with joy
when a moth is born.
After observing and waiting from spring (egg stage)
to summer (caterpillar stage)
winter cocoon and at lash a moth is born.
The students are full of joy and I'm full of joy.
A blush when self esteems buds into confidence out
his or her own ability to say I can do it.!
Lastly but not all when tears subsides after
I've comforted an felling or piches and pain.
When parents say Joe never was enthusiastic about
coming to school
before or I like the way you get the kids share their
opinions or ideas
or when students meet you in the hall and say I want
to be in your room next year
please may I? or I want to fail so I can stay in this
room.

These are the things that make it all worthwhile.
The other side extended away from the classroom
is when my daughter proudly says to her friend my
mother is a teacher.
My family states with pride she teaches.
I help others by being a teacher and bringing pride
and joy to others by being a teacher.
The students benefit
my daughter benefits my parents & family benefits
and I benefit.

I AM CONCERNED

I see teachers teaching for the
Future of the children's sake.
I see teachers who do nothing
But walk, talk, and fake.
I see teachers who come for
Only the money they make
I see teachers who teach for
Rewarding experiences and fulfillment
They take.
I am concerned as to whom of the above
Out numbers who
When I see the number that graduate.
I am concerned!

WHO KNOWS

Who knows how to build
a home?
Safe and warm from where evil roam.
And take care and nurture
a family,
and sing songs daily of joy and peace
happily.
And not worry about yesterday and
tomorrow,
and not hate nor entertain sorrow.
A bird knows . . . why don't we?

MY FRiEND

My friend talks when I listen
And listens when I talk
We know when to go
When the men in our lives call
My friend will let me know
When we can't agree
And it's ok when we eye to eye
Don't see.
I can call at three o'clock in the morning
And get a sleepy hello
I just need to talk and the time
Does not matter to my friend.

Asia Wrote

Dear Nanna Ma,
I love you to the bottom of my heart
I love to take care of you
And you love to take care of me
We both love to take care of each other
I love you and you love me.

I LOVE...

God
My children and family
Receiving red roses [one will do]
Long perfumed baths
Johnny Taylor
Sit by a body of water and watch it flow
Silk
To play cards
To try to sing
Teaching
Positive challenges
Pretty stem ware
Good books.

I LIKE . . .

Receiving cards for any occasion.
Hot peanut butter and jelly sandwiches.
Soft music and candle light dinners.
Good wines.
Traveling or going for a long walk on a warm rainy
day.
Long drives with Kenny G. playing.
Exploring untrodded wooded areas.
Helping others.
Window shopping
Pretty perfumes and matching undergarments.

Grabs My Mind

Candlesticks and glowing incense
Aromas, grabs my mind
Leave me open to all kind
Of pleasures which are now and then.
Sweet smelling flowers and beautiful insects
Their business grabs my mind.
Keeps me mindful
Of GOD's promises that provides and protects
Water movements and trailing water lilies,
Their order grabs my mind
Leaves me tranquil and very still
Then I watch GOD's plan at work.

You Made Me Wonder

Why did you leave here,
To leave me wondering, what I done wrong.
I was there for you, and you were never there.
You left me here to wonder
What it would be like if you were still here with me.
I wonder what it will be like for me from this day
forward.
I'm crying inside and I can't let you go,
But baby I will always remember you no matter,
No matter what happens to me,
I hurt inside you made me cry,
You made me scream, and you made me wonder.
I know its not the end.
One of these days, I will see you again
It may be soon, or it may be later
But when that day comes we will be together again.

Not Sure

He is this plastic person.
Who does all the politically
Correct and expected things.
Not brave enough yet to be himself
But tries defiantly to live up
To what someone else thinks is the way.
He stops his worth and defers to a myth
Of what should be, and slowly becomes synthetic
And not quite human.
Daily joy and peace
Happily,
And not worry about yesterday and
Tomorrow,
And not hate nor entertain any
Sorrow.

FEAR FEVER (SNAKES)

Snakes are not as dangerous as they seem.
They wiggle and turn, with a sense so keen.
When I asked Dustin why the fear fever.
He said, "I just don't like them."

LOVE IS THIS

Love is this, interactive, active
It is action. Love is non
Directed talk,
An adventure, an event, a smell,
a taste, a look, a smile, a slow walk.
Love is not whose right or wrong.
Love is this, a compromise, a sound, an embrace, a
stare,
A caress, a hug, a movement,
Parted lips,
A look, a care.

Im Excited . . .

By a warm misty breeze blowing across my face.
Warm glass of dry white wine
With slow jazzz
A tender kiss
A long hug

Im Fascinated By

The many wonders of nature,
Snakes,
Chess, and
A tall dark thin man
A sunset
A rainbow
A brilliant diamond
Life itself.

Being late is A Habit

Consistent lateness is a habit hidden under
elaborate excuses.
Lateness is punctuality challenged.
A behind the time zone. If you know you were late
yesterday,
leave at the same time today, for sure you will be late
again today!
Doing the same thing over and over again expecting
different results lends to madness or insane
arrogance.
An arrogance of feelings of importance.
Needs and personal interest are more important
than the ones to whom you are responsible.
There are influences that sometimes
you cannot control, but they don't occur every day.
Lateness is usual and customary to the habitual late
person.
Lateness is an adrenaline rush.
Therapy could be the key.
Lateness could be a disorder.

The Friendly
Gossiper's Interview

(Acting as though they want to be your friend)

How old are you . . .
Who are your people . . .
Where do you live . . .
Are you kin to . . .
Do you know . . .
Did you use to go with . . .
Did you use to be married to . . .
How many kids you got . . .
How old is your child . . .
What year did you graduate . . .
Where do you work . . .
(You then wonder what they are planning
to do with the information)
If you are not applying for anything, don't answer
these questions . . .
they are gathering information to spread !

p.s. **Intelligent people talk about ideas** . . . Average
people talk about things . . . Small people talk about
other people.

The Call

Hi Mrs. Williams, my name is Tekki. Could you
please
Tell your man to stop with the calls
And coming over here
He will not leave me alone.
I told him it was over
You done?
Now listen you did not call me when you were
sneaking
Around with him. I could have told you then.
Told you that you were not the first he cheated with,
Told you how this would end,
I cannot help you now.
I won't help!
I don't know what he told you but
he takes very good care of me and the children.
He won't leave me alone either. Trust me he does not
give up easily.
You do have a problem
So solve it.

Others

Gays, lesbians and other sexual orientations
Who are we to pass judgement on others sexuality
When this has been going on since the beginning of
time.
The bible speaks of the great kings and queens who
used their
Servants as they desired . . . and no one spoke out
against these events.

Jesus never denied their entrance to salvation by
describing
Who could enter into God's Kingdom:
acceptance and belief were the keys
Who are we as individuals and a society
to Change this?

YOU

The hurt that comes from the prosperity
That God bestows on another person makes the
pain so hard to bear
That we cannot bring ourselves to congratulate
or make notice of our brothers or sisters success.
We walk by seemingly not knowledgeable of the
person.

Instead we talk to another about the person behind
Their back. You think you have a reason for your
actions.
Remember there is a destiny that makes
us all brothers and sisters
and none of us walk our way alone.

All the mean spirited and ill wishes
We send into the lives of others
Finds its way back into our own lives.
How can God's choice to bless someone
Give YOU right to decide if the person is worthy and
be so painful to YOU

LONELY TEARS

As I sit here with tears
Rolling down my face.
As I sit here asking myself what wrong turn did I
make?
As I sit here wiping away the tears.
As I sit here asking myself what can
I do to change things and make them better? As I sit
here asking myself
Why can't I go to my closet and pull out my
childhood
And change everything about it.
As I sit here asking myself
Day after day after day as the tears
Roll down my face what I can do to make my life
better
But as I cry and hurt
Day and night
I finally realize there is nothing
I can do to change my past.

How to lose a Friend

One of the ways to lose a friend is to loan money.
They will find a reason to get angry with you
Which in turn will give them a reason to not pay you
back.
Some will use the saying you are not sympathetic to
their emotional situation
Such as "my rent is due," "a family member is sick," I
had to pay my bills."
A host of reasons not to pay you.
They will stop answering your calls. You may get
charged with harassment if you ask for your money
more than twice.
"Stop bothering me about that lil ol money" is what
you will be told.
You have now lost a friend.

Believe

If you believe within your heart
You will know that no one can change the path
That you must go
Believe what you feel and know you are right
because
The time will come when you take ownership of
your belief
And follow your heart.
Believe that you can go on, believe you can better
yourself
Set your standards and goals high
Believe you will get there
Believe in that feeling in your heart and follow it.
Believe that feeling is God speaking to you.
Believe.

WAS NOT WAS IS

Was not man, beast, fowl, plants terrorist,
The world as we know it
Was large beast, cities, land profiles, species terroe
The world as we know it.
Is man, animal, water plants, landscapes, high rise
building,
Crime, terrorist.
The world as we know it
Is to be unknown
The world as we know it.

If God brings you to it, he will bring you through it.
Happy moments, praise God
Difficult moments, seek God
Quiet moments, worship God
Painful moments, trust God
Every moment, thank God.

WHAT IS DEATH

What is Death?
Death is a transfer of energy!
From a blossom to a flower; from water to ice.
It doesn't matter how nice,
How young, how old or how lovely.
What is Death?
It is a transfer of energy!
There's nothing to weep. That energy is
Here to keep. Our love ones are not gone.
Please there is no need to moan.
For energy CANNOT be destroyed!
It will always be employed.
What is Death?
It is the transfer of energy! It is the
Escaping of one form of energy to another . . .
The form we may not know. But be sure . . .
Life passes on to something that will surely start to
Grow!

Waited

I've waited so long for Mr. Right.
He came my way
Oh what a grand day
We looked into each other's eyes
We exchanged hellos and no good byes

I've waited for so long now I'm filled
With joy and my heart sealed
Time has stood still. I waited for your return
I see visions and glances of all sort.
No you for so long and now for so short.

LADAKA

Lady the strong personality. A plan for everything.
Exact with high values and standards. Kind and full of care
for those who have less freehearted to her sister, nieces and nepfews.
Doing as if they were her own . . . thats the mother in her
Strong brave caring

Alicia the wonderful mother to her children
with strict values set by her life experiences.
emotional and very sensitive to family events
internal pain from childhood experience
let go be happy use as a guide to not do
strong brave loving

Debbie the wise wisdom gain from life's paths she took
Willing and ready to take on events
That come upon the family caretaker for the animals
So profound, take heed and listen hides pain so as
not to cause others concern
Strong brave wise

Asia grandchild, the angel God sent the family
Pretty, caring and loving
the children doctor

Kyle the first grandchild, first boy to the family
Loved by all
Funny, very smart and creative
The lawyer or politician

Amari the professor
Smart and a thinker
Inventor doctor

The mother who loves each one for their uniqueness
Love each differently because you are all different
Love you all because you are all mine
Not knowing how to show the love she never
received
Made many mistakes trying
The most important has and always will be is "What
my children think of me."